C000194275

STEPHEN BERESFORD

Stephen Beresford is a writer for stage and screen. He trained at RADA and his first play *The Last of the Haussmans* opened at the National Theatre, London, starring Julie Walters in 2012 to great critical and commercial success. His stage adaptation of Ingmar Bergman's *Fanny & Alexander* was first performed at The Old Vic, London, in 2018.

His first screenplay was *Pride* (2014), directed by Matthew Warchus. It premiered at Cannes Film Festival where it closed Directors' Fortnight. The film won three British Independent Film Awards (including Best British Film) and was nominated in four further categories, received the South Bank Show Award for Best British Film, and was nominated for BAFTA Best British Film, Golden Globe Best Motion Picture and London Critic's Circle British Film of the Year. Stephen won the BAFTA Award for Outstanding Debut.

Stephen Beresford

THREE KINGS

NICK HERN BOOKS
London
www.nickhernbooks.co.uk

A Nick Hern Book

Three Kings first published in Great Britain in 2020 as a paperback original by Nick Hern Books Limited, The Glasshouse, 49a Goldhawk Road, London W12 8QP

Three Kings copyright © 2020 Stephen Beresford
Introduction copyright © 2020 Matthew Warchus

Stephen Beresford has asserted his moral right to be identified as the author of this work

Cover photograph of Andrew Scott by Leigh Keily, Camera Press London

Designed and typeset by Nick Hern Books, London
Printed in the UK by Mimeo Ltd, Huntingdon, Cambridgeshire PE29 6XX

A CIP catalogue record for this book is available from the British Library

ISBN 978 1 84842 977 2

Introduction
Matthew Warchus, director

The *Old Vic: In Camera* series was devised as a fundraising experiment in the midst of the 2020 pandemic. Having spent innumerable hours over many weeks on Zoom conference calls, it occurred to me that the platform might provide an opportunity to share socially distanced performances (actors only ever appearing in their own single frames) with a geographically distant lockdown audience. With the theatre being closed, and with most of our staff on furlough, the plays would need to be presented in a stripped back way with very little *mise en scène* – and so I decided to spin the staging of each show 180 degrees and use the empty auditorium as a background, providing a poignant visual context for the productions.

Three Kings, which arrived out of the blue, whilst Andrew Scott and I were searching for something for him to perform, was the first monologue of the *In Camera* series and the first piece to be written specially for the format. I'm hugely grateful to Stephen for essentially donating the world premiere of this superbly written and very personal play to The Old Vic at such a critical time. And equally indebted to Andrew for navigating a very strange form of theatre (live but with no apparent audience!) with such panache and for supporting the theatre via his mesmerising performances.

I love this play. It's a super example of the paradox that a specific and personal story can have wide resonance. Can we love (and forgive) what disappoints us? How do we manage to be kind, natural and honest, in love and life, even whilst accumulating bruises and scars? These are challenges we all face. And tricks we will struggle to fathom.

Three Kings was first performed at The Old Vic, London, on 3 September 2020, as part of the *Old Vic: In Camera* series, a new artistic initiative of socially distanced performances, all streamed live from the iconic Old Vic stage with the empty auditorium as a backdrop.

The cast and production team was as follows:

Cast	Andrew Scott
Director	Matthew Warchus
Design	Rob Howell
Lighting	Tim Lutkin
Broadcast Sound & Video	Simon Baker & Jay Jones
Associate Director	Katy Rudd
Associate Lighting	Sarah Brown
Stage Manager	Maria Gibbons
Deputy Stage Manager	Emma Tooze
Head of Lighting	Andrew Stuttard
Camera Operators	Avril Cook, Karina Olson, Josh Reeves
Sound & Video Operator	James Percival
Production Manager	Dominic Fraser
Head of Wardrobe	Fiona Lehmann
Set Construction	Aran Morrison & Karina Olson
Sound & Video Equipment	Stage Sound Services

Special thanks to Zoom.

Thanks to all of The Old Vic Staff.

For my sister, Joanna

1

PATRICK – *when we see him – is probably shabby. A lifetime of bar-hopping might be suggested. First, though, we just see his hands – camera over the shoulder – and three pound coins, spread out at equal distances in a straight line on the surface. At some point, the camera moves so that he can be fully visible.*

'Three coins. Three kings. *Tres reyes.*

'*Uno. Dos. Tres…*

'This is a hotel-lobby trick. A café trick. This is one for the bars – '

PATRICK *puts the coins next to each other so they're touching.*

'Master this, and you'll have drinks all night – you'll make an impact.'

Maybe we can see PATRICK*'s face now.*

Making an impact, I'm about to learn, is one of my father's favourite themes.

'There are rules about bars, Patrick. The first, and most important – is *never* sit down.'

I'm eight years old.

This is the first time we have properly met.

My mother – mindful of the fact that none of his other promises has escalated into an actual appearance – has kept this visit a secret from me.

And so – today – it's a surprise to find myself alone with him in the dining room. Alone with my father for the very first time.

'You'll never make an impact sitting on your arse,' he says.

I nod, because… well, I'm eight. And I think that probably sounds about right.

'There are only three types of people who sit down in bars – women, priests, and cripples.'

He taps the desk – returning my attention to the coins.

'This king – the first king – he can be touched and moved.'

Demonstrates by moving the coin around the counter.

'This king – the second king – can be touched but never moved.'

Points at the coin but neither touches nor moves it.

'This king – the third king – can be moved but never touched.'

I'm staring at him. I should be staring at the coins but I can't seem to break the gaze.

He's in a corduroy blazer, pink shirt, silk tie, pocket square. He smells of sandalwood. The smoke from a Dunhill cigarette is twisting itself down between his fingers. The red-and-gold packet – which to me seems impossibly chic – is lying on the table by the coins.

'Princess Margaret smokes these. I saw her stealing an ashtray once in Lismore Castle. Look at the coins.'

My sister remembers him. She is four years older than me. She remembers when he lived with us – in a string of rented apartments in the centre of Dublin – He could only flourish, he said, in Georgian architecture…

It was a time of high windows – she tells me – of the beginning of my mother's 'episodes'. A time of debt collectors, and exile, and escape.

'How did you *meet*?' I would ask my mother –

'I was pretty,' she says. And not without defensiveness.

'But – what did he say?'

'He was struck – that was the word he used. He was dazzled…'

She appraises herself in the mirror – a stray lock of hair.

'I was a snappy dresser, then – and not like the other girls. He recognised my coat – the quality of it.'

I want to know if my father is staying in Dublin.

I try to imagine how Princess Margaret would make such an enquiry.

'Are you staying in Dublin these days?'

'I'm abroad,' he says. 'I'm into something at the moment. Something quite interesting… some fella I met at The Shelbourne Hotel. It's an opportunity.'

'What?'

'It's complicated. It has the potential to be extremely lucrative – if people are imaginative enough – brave enough… if they keep their nerve.'

He looks at me to see whether or not I am worthy of elaboration.

'Something to do with smoked fish.'

He gestures at the table.

'This king can be touched and moved. This king can touched but not moved. This king can be moved but not touched.

'Any bar in the world you can try this in. It's a universal form of communication. What languages do you speak?'

'French?' I lie.

'French isn't really a language. It's a series of vocalised evasions. With French you can pretty much say anything you like – it's just a question of noodling down your nose… If that's the sort of thing that interests you, you'd be far better taking up the bassoon.'

I'm staring at him.

'Arabic is a proper language for a gentleman. It's lyrical without being effeminate.'

He shifts the coins ever so slightly – still touching,
still together – and then he says something –
I assume in Arabic –

'*Ana ash ala couscousak.*

'Do you know what that means?'

I don't.

'It means – "I will shit in your couscous"…

'It's a punchy phrase… Never use it in Algeria.'

His smoke is filling the room. Hours after he's gone I
shall smell it – on my clothes and my hair.

'Spanish, of course, is your language.'

He says this as though it were obvious – but there's a
defensiveness there. A caution.

'I suppose your mother never told you about that.

'Your dark hair? Your brown eyes? – That's your
Spanish ancestry. My ancestry.

'There's more to you than your mother, you know.
Your great-grandfather laid all the electric cables
across Spain. Married a Spanish girl.

'House in Madrid, estate in Málaga… They made
their own sherry. And I don't mean in a vat in the
kitchen. They had peasants – workers. They bottled it
for their own consumption… Two of their sons
became cardinals.

'Don't think *you're* getting any money, though. It's
gone. The fascists took it. The only way you'll ever

get any money is by being smart. By living on your wits. Like me. By learning the rules of life – and by not allowing yourself to be fucked over.'

He looks at his watch. I'm frightened. I'm frightened of him.

'This king can be touched and moved. This king can be touched but not moved. This king can be moved but not touched.'

I stare at the coins, willing myself to understand.

'The trick – the game… is to get this king – (*The first*.) between these two… To put him in the middle.'

I stare.

What?

'This king can be touched and moved. This king can be touched but not moved. This king can be moved but not touched.'

I put my finger down on the first king – the one I can touch and move.

I wander it aimlessly around the table.

I put my finger down on the second king – the one that can be touched but not moved.

I look back at him.

I can't do this, I think. I'm going to fail.

But then he smiles. A broad, warm smile – and he places a hand on my shoulder. And I am aware, in that second, that this is the first time – at least within memory – that he has ever touched me.

And I know – because I can feel it – that this is the beginning of a whole new chapter.

My father – dark-haired, like I am – and me. The two of us.

And scary though he is – intimidating though he is – I know, in this moment, he *will be* my father now. And we will develop an easy, natural way – almost offhand – almost banal. And it will not just be my mother and my sister from now on. It will be him too. And I will change because of it.

'Put the first king between the other two... Put the first king between the other two...'

I hope that this will impress him – this diligence, this effort of concentration. But he's looking around the room.

'That tobacco jar used to be mine,' he says. 'The blue one. It's Bristol Glass. It's actually quite valuable.'

I shuffle the coin about for a minute.

'Is it a trick?' I ask.

'Of course it's a trick,' he says. 'I'm teaching you a trick. What else are we doing here?'

'But is it impossible?'

'If it were impossible...' he says, 'would I be wasting my time on it?

'If it were impossible… would it have saved my life in a fish market in Essaouira?'

The hand has left the shoulder now.

I look down at the table.

'Does your mother still take pills?'

'Yes – '

'For her nerves?'

I don't know what they're for but I nod.

'Stupid woman.'

He doesn't say that, but he thinks it.

I can see.

I can see his contempt for her.

And in a tiny act of betrayal – shaking her off me so easily, so faithlessly – I mimic him.

Tentatively, I move the first king around the polished table, and edge him delicately between the second and third.

I look back.

He sighs.

He has none of the pleasure people normally have when you fail at their game. He has no glint of triumph – no rush of success.

'The third king – ?' He says.

'Moved but not touched.' I say.

'But you did touch it. You touched it with the edge of the first.'

I try again, and it's true. I did.

'Let's call this a test,' he says. 'See if you can work it out. See if you can work it out, and if you can – I'll reward you.'

'How?'

'With a prize.'

I can feel my way through this now.

'This will be our schtick,' I think. Gamesmanship. Challenges. A jokey, fun relationship where puzzles are set.

A good-natured rivalry.

This is the nature of fathers, I think. It must be. This is their way.

'What will the prize be?' I ask.

He's slipping his cigarettes into the pocket of his blazer.

'If you can solve it – ' he says, 'If you can prove to me that you've solved it – '

His eyes are already focused on the door –

'Then I will come back and see you one day.'

My belly flips over. It drops. My whole weight seems to press into the soles of my feet.

'But… aren't you coming back?'

'Not unless you can solve it,' he says.

I try to smile.

'Think of it as an intelligence test. I need to see what you're made of. I need to test your mettle. I'm not wasting my time on a mental defective.'

He laughs – and in a second act of treachery – this time against myself – I join in.

'You're not a mental defective, I take it?'

'No!' I say, pretending to enjoy the joke enormously.

'No…'

After he's gone I vomit.

I have diarrhoea for three days.

My mother seems to blame me for his appearance. 'What did you expect?' Goes back to calling him 'your ex-father'.

I am sixteen before I speak to him again.

Two years before that, I learn how to solve The Three Kings. A boy at my school has picked it up at Leopardstown Racecourse.

I have my own tastes now – or like to think I have.

I go to foreign films and I have a poster of *Betty Blue* on my wall.

When I finally track him down – it's a phone number – a foreign number. In Switzerland, it turns out... The home of millionaires.

I call from a phone box so as not to upset my mother.

There's a party going on in the background – and a singalong which – somehow – couldn't be anything other than German.

I imagine the red-and-white-checked tablecloths and the inevitable swinging of steins...

'Yes?' He says.

He seems bad tempered to be called to the phone – and more than a little cagey. But I already have a strategy – offhand, effortless, sophisticated...

I demonstrate this by not even saying hello – just launching into it.

'I have solved The Three Kings.' I say.

I'm also smoking a Silk Cut – which is fogging up the phone box – but which adds to the atmosphere of masculine bonhomie.

'Who is this?'

I absorb his question – or the blow of it – with a laugh – a noise I've picked up from other men – a kind of bark that indicates humour without having to actively participate in it.

'Your coin trick,' I say. 'Your backstreet enterprise – The Three Kings – I've solved it.

'It's Patrick.' I say –

'Patrick…?'

There's a long silence, and then – after what may or may not have been a mumbled conversation with someone else – he laughs down the phone – and I realise, for the first time, quite how drunk he is.

'Patrick – ' he says. 'Patrick…

'Listen. You've got a stepmother.'

'*What?*' I say –

I can hear a mumbling, then – and a shriek of laughter –

'Only she's far too young and beautiful to be called "Stepmother", so don't.

'Do you know where your sister's living now?'

'Erm… yes…' I say.

'I want to send her a picture.'

'Of what?'

'Oh… Yes… you've got a little brother, actually.

'Quite a character. Very bonny. The absolute spit of his old man.'

And then he says –

It's funny, because I've replayed this next thing, so many times – and I've reached so many different conclusions… Had he forgotten who he was speaking to? Was it deliberate? Was it a joke?

And then he says –

'The longed-for son and heir.'

And he puts down the phone.

2

'I have never understood the enthusiasm people have for dying by the sea.

'I like the sea. I like the sucking of waves on shingle – I'm not… This isn't a condemnation of the poetic principles of nature.'

I have no idea why I am speaking like this.

I'm looking around the café. It has tiles on the walls in yellow and blue. A scene – like a mural – stretching across them. I think it's a bull facing down a matador, but half of it's hidden behind a fridge.

'This is one of the more… authentic places,' he says. And I can't quite detect whether that's a boast or an apology.

I have a brandy in front of me – which, I'm aware, has raised some eyebrows at ten o'clock in the morning – but since I've been brought here on the business of death, I appear to have been excused –

At least by him.

A television, above the bar, is showing football.

There are little plates of octopus and potato skewered onto toothpicks. A neon sign in the window – 'Estrella'.

He taps my hand and, nods over at the glass counter.

'Don't touch the ham.'

His name is Dennis.

'I was a friend of your father's,' he says. 'In as much as he…'

'Had friends?'

'Allowed people in.' Dennis replies.

He seems pleased with that – and he lets it sit there between us for a moment.

Dennis has lived here for almost fourteen years. He is a leading light among the expatriate community. He offers all kinds of services – mortgage broking, naturalisation, currency exchange.

'Not that he was unpopular…' he adds. 'Oh, far from it. He was always a very…'

I can see that the dangling of unfinished sentences is going to be Dennis's style.

'Especially with the ladies, of course.

'I helped him with all his difficulties.'

'You mean prison?' I say.

'I gave him advice. I advised him. Especially about the divorces. His will. There were – this being Spain – the inevitable land and property issues…'

He's obviously going to gloss over my father's brief but significant criminal career, so I say it again.

'Did you help him when he was sent to prison?'

'He was incarcerated, yes. Briefly. In Madrid. I gave advice to his wife...'

'You must remind me – ' I say, 'would that have been Barbara?'

'Barbara?'

'Barbara. An older lady. Made a lot of money in care homes, I think...'

'No...' he says. He looks troubled for a moment. 'I think Barbara might have been before my time. This was Concepción.'

'Concepción?'

'A younger person. Very pretty. At one time she was a stewardess for Jet Blue.'

'Oh.'

I've never heard of Jet Blue. I try not to make that a reflection on Concepción, but I'm not entirely sure I succeed.

'And did she last the course?' I say.

'No... She was a little... excitable. She didn't take too kindly to him being carted off like that. It was rather a shock.'

'It must have been.'

'Extremely heavy-handed – but then, that's the guarda civil for you. Frankly, I can't think what was gained by it. Apprehending him, like that, at the

Royal Málaga Yacht Club… Parading him past the buffet in handcuffs…'

Dennis is exercised by this miscarriage of justice so he's keen to change the subject.

'You've been here before!' He says, brightly. 'Three months ago!'

I fold the napkin.

'My sister told me he was dying and so I came. I came and visited him.'

'I wasn't here.'

Dennis seems genuinely saddened by that.

'I was visiting the mainland – for a client in concrete.'

'I didn't expect to be back again so soon.' I say.

He pats my hand.

'That trip must have been good for you,' he says. 'And him.

'Closure.'

He says the word as though he's only recently come across it – and perhaps he has.

His wife may have used it in front of him. Or his daughter.

I can see them sitting on a terrace, sharing a jug of sangria. Dennis loves his family – I know that from spending a few minutes with him.

I see them everywhere – men who love their families. I have an antenna for it.

I see them young – pushing swings and standing outside of schools. I see them old – in booths at restaurants – at graduation ceremonies...

My father was not such a man, I think.

And neither am I.

'He was completely exonerated.

'They sent him all the way back to Ireland and he was released. A full acquittal.'

'I know,' I say.

'He may have owed a great deal of money – he may have been less than assiduous with his VAT, but nothing he did was *strictly speaking* criminal. The whole exercise was a gross waste of public money.'

I half-notice that I'm gesturing for another brandy.

'Just before we run away with this idea of my father as Steve Biko, Dennis – I have to interject with a little story – do you mind? It's about my sister and her children.'

'Oh yes?'

'You see, my sister, being soft-hearted, thought that once he was released, he would spend a few days in the city – get to know his grandchildren. Can you imagine their excitement, Dennis? They were fast asleep when he finally got back, but they'd made a huge banner – "Welcome Granddad"… and stuck it over his bedroom door – Obviously, if they'd asked my advice – or even yours – we could have told the little mites not to waste their crayons, but there it is… He was gone the next morning, Dennis. Left before dawn. Just scribbled down a note to my sister and vanished before anyone was up.

'"*I have to get back to Spain. I'll see the kids another time.*"

'And then on the back –

'"*Not sure about 'Granddad'.*"

'And underneath that – because who can resist a wild, romantic postscript –

'"*I've fallen in love!*"'

Dennis nods.

'I take it that wasn't Concepción,' I say.

'No…' says Dennis.

'That would have been Trish.'

I can see our conversation is taking its toll.

He searches the table, as though Trish – or some traces of her biography – might be found there.

'Trish runs a bar on the other side of the island. I think there may have been a certain amount of crossover between her and Concepción.'

We settle into silence.

'I think perhaps we'd better get down to business...
For some time your father spoke about donating his
body to medical science.'

I let out a short but impressive screech – Even in
death, he has the ability to surprise me.

'Unfortunately he never got round to completing the
paperwork, so that course of action...'

'There *was* a will.'

He pulls out some papers in Spanish – pink and
yellow.

'I see.'

'But it was somewhat out of date.'

He takes a sip of his Fanta.

'Unfortunately, Patrick – in Spain, at least – a new
will must be notarised and filed with the appropriate
clerk...'

'I'm guessing he never got round to that, either,
Dennis.'

'No. He did not.'

Dennis is more businesslike now. I feel as though his
brief foray into my family has besmirched him in
some way. He longs to get back to that terrace. To
Mrs Dennis. To nice people who treat each other with
respect.

'There's no good way to say this, Patrick, but since
there was no new will, the few assets your father

still held, will revert to the original beneficiary, named in…'

'1992.'

'And that was…'

'Sonja.'

'Sonja…'

'Third wife.'

'No one else is mentioned. No instruction with regard to personal effects. Nothing. It's a very short document.'

I nod.

He nods.

A Spanish striker scores on the screen.

'If you like I can drop you at his house on the way to the airport. If there's anything there you'd like to take – a keepsake – a memento…'

I smile.

Dennis is a good man. A kind man. I shouldn't have tortured him with that story about my sister's children.

'May I just say –

'Your father spoke of you. Quite often, in fact… He was… well… It's my honest belief… as his friend… that he was proud of you.'

I nod.

'Both of you. I'm not just saying that.'

The football has now become an advert. A woman with red hair is dancing with a shampoo bottle.

'I believe that he was proud of both his children. He said so – quite often.

'"I have two exceptional children."'

'Three,' I say, quietly.

'I'm sorry?'

'There were three of us.' I say. 'My father... He met a woman somewhere in Switzerland... they had a son. My half-brother.'

I don't want to hurt Dennis. I don't want to brutalise him any further. I don't want to shatter his view of what a father is – or should be. I hate myself.

'Three...' says Dennis.

'Three.'

A little silence.

'Do you know where he is – Your brother?'

I shake my head.

'Don't you think you ought to tell him...?'

'I believe they fell out. I still haven't... I can't... I've left a lot of messages. I think I have a very old number.'

And, for some reason I hear myself say –

'I'm sorry.'

Beat.

Outside in the street, I listen to messages.

There are three from someone I lived with for two years, then left without explanation.

The message is a familiar one – it is a list of my faults – and because all of them are true, I listen humbly and without emotion – like a penance.

I have been reckless with money.

I am emotionally unavailable.

I have lied – and not just about big things like bills and credit-card debts – but about small things.

Why would somebody lie about a coal delivery?

Why would somebody lie about how much a shirt cost?

I drink my way across the island.

With almost four hours to go until my plane leaves, I light on an idea – I find what I'm looking for quite easily – A bar. On the far side of the island. Called Trisha's.

It is a much larger establishment than I had anticipated.

There is a dance floor.

Potted palms.

Trish is unmistakable.

She is in her early sixties, with blonde hair.

She turns from the bar, as I enter – and so too does a middle-aged man, who is seated at a table near her.

She gestures for him to sit down.

She's fine.

She walks slowly towards me, with an expression I can only describe as hostile.

She seems to recognise me as well.

Perhaps – although I doubt it – she has seen a photograph.

'I'm not serving,' she says.

Which is a surprise because her T-shirt tells us in glitter, no less, that it is:

'Prosecco O'Clock.'

'Hello…' I say.

It's only as I start to speak that I realise quite how drunk I am – how red my face is. How hot.

'Hello, I'm – '

'I know who you are,' she says.

'Yes,' I say. 'And I know who you are.

'I think you knew my father.' I say.

I realise how close we're standing – How strongly she smells of perfume – how strongly I might smell of gin –

'Your father…' she says –

'Your father was the kindest, the gentlest, the humblest and most beautiful spirit I ever met.'

I'm a little surprised by this description.

I sway in the doorway.

'He…

'He was a saint.'

It occurs to me that she might be referring to someone else – some other serial monogamist – some other compulsive womaniser who wove his way across the island.

'It was because of you, young man, that he lost everything. His patents, his businesses – his medical licence…'

'His *patents*?'

'For the aquatic car.'

I can't say a word.

Only move my mouth.

'And I think the way you treated him was absolutely disgusting.'

She turns and makes her way, slowly, back to the bar.

I can see no way of escaping while holding on to my dignity, and so – for reasons I will never quite understand – I brace myself in the doorway and execute a slow but deliberate bow to her retreating back.

'*Gracias*, Trisha,' I say.

'*Muchas gracias*.'

3

It is a tiny house.

It is also squalid and filthy.

There is a terrible little yard where weeds and filth and rubbish have accumulated for many years.

There is a dog chained up somewhere nearby – howling.

The wind is gritty and relentless – although we're only halfway up the side of the mountain.

It is hot – even in November.

The room in which he both lives and sleeps has an appalling smell. He appears to have been living on Sugar Puffs.

He will take no medication.

'I have no business with doctors – ' he says.

Big pharma has become a favourite topic now – 'Disease is a racket.'

He will cure his cancer with soursop fruit.

He has read it on the internet.

'Most diseases are generated in laboratories,' he says, 'so that we can be charged for the cure.'

That strikes me as something that he, as a lover of enterprise, ought to approve of – but I say nothing.

'Do you think he suffered?'

I am telling all this or a version of it in a pub in Bristol.

Across from me is a young man with a high-visibility jacket over his sweatshirt, and a yellow hard hat hanging from his chair.

He is so gripped by the story that he has scarcely touched his pint.

I, on the other hand, am well into my third gin and tonic.

He has already wept.

He is my brother.

I am surprised to find that he is good looking – I don't know why.

It has amused us that we are both named Patrick – after him.

'I expect he thought of you as an upgrade. A correction.'

This upsets him and he shakes his head and reaches for my arm.

'I prefer to go by Paddy, anyway.'

His mother was an ordinary English girl who happened to land a job cleaning chalets. She was much younger than him.

He had swept her away.

For the first two years of her marriage, he had told her that he was a Spanish count.

'Are you sure he said "count"?

'Take away a letter and he might even be telling the truth.'

He laughs at this.

He laughs easily.

I find myself tremendously drawn to him – his innocence, his open nature.

He is greeted warmly when we come into the pub – and he introduces me with a great beaming smile.

'This is my brother. From Ireland.'

He has no need to impress. He takes a little gentle teasing when he declines to sit with his friends – and I find myself wondering – how a man can be so natural in himself.

I think he is well-liked.

It has taken years to find him.

The news of our father's death is a terrible blow – they had parted on poor terms.

He is inconsolable when I speak of his death – but he is determined to hear everything about my visit – the last visit to the house on the mountain, to the island where he lived.

I tell him that we too had not spoken for many many years.

He nods. Relieved, I think.

'He was an intensely difficult man, Paddy.'

I am aware that every detail I provide seems to land with him – like a kindness.

'My sister told me he was dying – and so I took a plane to go and see him.'

'I would love to meet your sister,' he says.

'My sister.'

He laughs at the realisation of this.

His hair is dark too, his eyes…

'Appalling people on this island,' he said. 'Common.'

He introduces me to one or two of his acquaintances – I get the impression that they are mostly used to drive him around – or to run errands.

One in particular – Pete – seems so enthralled, that he is impervious to insult or injury.

'Pete – ' he says, while Pete smiles away in front of us, 'is an example of how the British have deteriorated… From Shakespeare to Palmerston to Pete. A sunburned halfwit in denim shorts.'

Pete describes my father as 'A proper character'.

At night things are different.

He is frightened.

Unsure of where he is.

He cries out and reaches for me – sometimes he weeps.

It takes him forever to get into bed – and even when
he does, he gets up at least four times to pace about –
and to check the positions of certain objects.

The moon illuminates the filthy yard.

'What's happening?' He screams.

'What is it?'

I try to quiet him by rubbing his foot – the only part
of him I can reach without leaving my little camp
bed in the corner of the room.

Neither of us has mentioned – since I arrived – that
in a series of emails five years ago, we have traded
such blows – such appalling insults – that no
ordinary person could have recovered.

He has told me that I was only born so that my sister
wouldn't be bored.

He has told me that he never loved my mother and
never intended to stay.

He has told me that I am him – the same as him –
and that anything my imagination has created is his –
his gift to me.

That should be remembered.

That should be honoured.

I have told him that he is a cheat.

And a liar.

I have told him that he has given me nothing.

I have told him my sister hates him.

That her children laugh at him – all of us laugh at him. Together.

I have told him that I will never see him again.

And yet…

A little silence.

He shivers with fear for most of the night – whimpers like a child.

'Did your mother take her own life?'

'We don't know. My sister found her.'

A long muffled sobbing into the pillow follows this enquiry.

Later –

'Ireland is a terrible country. Why aren't you ashamed of it?'

He's fierce now. Furious.

'Oh I am,' I say, 'every *Eurovision* I'm inconsolable.'

And then he lets out a roar of pain.

The next morning he shows me a photograph album – things I've never seen, never knew existed.

Himself – young, rangy. Leaning against a bicycle – a sort of defiance in the eyes.

No friends.

No groups.

His parents – in black and white.

'Dead before you arrived.'

A tiny little couple – posed, uncomfortably – outside the entrance of UCD.

'Who are all these?' I ask.

A grand house on the Retiro Park in Madrid.

An estate in Málaga.

A family – all in white linen – pages and pages of them.

He doesn't know their names.

But he places his hand, lovingly, onto the page – and rests it there.

The last entry is the most surprising.

Ireland. Six photographs in Polaroid colour. The west, by the look of it. Landscapes. No figures.

Beautiful.

What was this? A lonesome holiday? The bicycle appears in two of them.

'You can't love what disappoints you,' he says. 'Can you?'

And then –

Before I answer that... because I *can* answer it.

He says something I never expected to hear – and in a voice I have never heard him use.

'Will you pray for me?'

My brother – Paddy – is weeping.

I rest my hand on his.

A barmaid – who knows and likes him – brings us both another drink.

On the house.

She squeezes his shoulder as she leaves, and she offers me a smile.

'I have a son,' he says.

He cannot look up.

'I have a boy.

'He's ten.'

I think for a moment he's going to pull out his phone and show me a photograph, but he's finding a tissue.

'I'm no better,' he says. 'I'm no better than he was.'

He cannot meet my eye.

'I don't get on with his mother. She's a fucking lunatic. It's not my fault if she can't get herself together. I tried.'

'Of course you did.' I say – with no justification whatsoever.

'She moves him around,' he says, 'I don't know what she tells him about me. How can I know?'

Before I go, I give him the photograph album.

He squeezes me so tightly, so painfully, that I cannot move.

'You'll come and see me again – ' he says.

He's bubbling over with ideas and plans and schemes – he will come and meet my sister, and her children – he will visit Ireland – he will visit Spain – We will meet his son –

'You'll come again.'

He says.

'You will come back.'

He's still gripping me.

'You'll come and see me again.'

I cannot leave him, I think. Not like this.

'Three coins.' I say. 'Three kings. *Tres reyes.*'

I reach into my pocket and pull out three coins, which I place onto the bar beside us.

'*Uno. Dos. Tres…*

'This king can be touched and moved. This king can be touched but not moved. This king can be moved but not touched.'

He stares at me.

Bewildered.

'What is it?' He says.

'It's a test,' I say.

'This king has to get between these two. You have to put him in the middle.'

He stares at the table then looks at me.

And I show him. I show him exactly how it is done.

PATRICK *takes the middle king and holds it down – touched but not moved – and then, moving and touching the first king, he knocks it against the second, causing the third to skid off away from the others. He slides the second king between the other two.*

'There,' I say.

'The force of the one ricochets through the other two.

'That should save you a bit of time.'

He smiles.

He is disproportionately impressed.

'Who taught you that?' He asks.

'My mother.'

A little silence.

I say goodbye and leave – And as I leave, I can hear him –

'You'll come back – won't you?

'You've got my number.

'You'll come back, Patrick.'

He is telling the others –

'That was my brother. You'll all meet him. He'll be back. You can meet him when he comes back.'

A little silence.

That must have been four years ago.

Five, maybe.

Little silence.

Dear Father –

We are the breakers of promises.

We are the fakes and the fantasists –

We are the exaggerators of facts at dinner parties.

We are the fools.

We are the liars who cannot – even if we wanted to – reveal the true price of anything.

We are those upon whom it is impossible to place your trust.

Look down on us.

We are the charming.

We are those who owe money.

We are faithless, and dead to shame.

Except when we *are* ashamed – except at night and alone – except then.

We want to be kind.

And natural.

And easy.

We believe that we could perhaps be honest in love.

In life.

If only someone would teach us that trick.

Have mercy on us.

Father.

Have mercy.

And if we may just stretch your indulgence…

(That, after all, is our particular skill.)

Silence.

Forgive us.

Tim F

RESIDE...
ALIEN

Quentin Crisp
explains it all

NICK HERN BOOKS
London
www.nickhernbooks.co.uk
in association with

FatBloke Productions

A Nick Hern Book

Resident Alien first published in this revised edition
in Great Britain in 2001 as a paperback original
by Nick Hern Books Limited, 14 Larden Road,
London W3 7ST, in association with FatBloke Productions

First published in 1999, reprinted twice.

Typeset by Country Setting, Kingsdown, Kent CT14 8ES
Printed and bound in Great Britain by Biddles Ltd, Guildford

ISBN 1 85459 657 8

A CIP catalogue record for this book is available from
the British Library

Resident Alien

Resident Alien is produced by Sarah Earl,
David Johnson, Fat Bloke Productions and Brass,
with the following cast and crew:

QUENTIN   Bette Bourne

Director   Tim Fountain
Designer   Julian McGowan
Lighting Designer   Sid Higgins

Based on the original Bush Theatre Production
directed by Mike Bradwell, which opened there on
10 November 1999, press night 12 November 1999.

BETTE BOURNE
(Quentin)

Bette Bourne has acted in most of the leading theatres in
Britain. He has worked in Repertory, The West End and
the Old Vic alongside noted actors Sir Ian McKellen,
Dame Sybil Thorndike and Simon Callow and with such
directors as Trevor Nunn, Maria Aitken, Philip Prowse,
Mike Bradwell and Adrian Noble. Over the past decade
he has been lauded for his work with Neil Bartlett both
as the castrato-diva star of *Sarrasine* and as Lord Henry
Wooton in *The Picture of Dorian Gray*. In 1995 he won
the Manchester Evening News Award for his
performance as Lady Bracknell in *The Importance of
Being Earnest* (a credit he shares in common with
Quentin Crisp). Bette is also famous for his celebrated
queer comedy ensemble Bloolips, with whom he won
two OBIES. He received his third OBIE for *Resident
Alien* at the New York Theatre Workshop in 2001.

TIM FOUNTAIN
(Writer/Director)

Writing credits include: *Harold's Day* (BAC), *Once in a
Blue Moon* (Coventry Belgrade Studio), *Tchaikovsky in
the Park* (Bridewell Theatre), *The Last Bus From
Bradford* (Drill Hall and Chelsea Centre, London),
Resident Alien (Bush Theatre, London/New York Theatre
Workshop, New York, USA; also broadcast on BBC
Radio 3) and *Quentin Crisp,* a biography (to be published
in 2001).

His directing credits include *Puppetry Of The Penis*
(Whitehall Theatre, London and National tour),

*Grandmotherfucker (*Assembly Rooms, Edinburgh),
Harold's Day and *These Childish Things* (Hull Truck
Theatre, Hull), *Antigone* (Birmingham Rep Studio), *Once
in A Blue Moon* (Coventry Belgrade Studio), *Last Bus
From Bradford* (Chelsea Centre).

Television credits: *Arriverderrci Barnsley* (Channel Four
Sitcom Festival, Riverside Studios), *Bob and Margaret*
(Channel Four/Nelvana/Comedy Central USA) for which
he was one of the principal writers on Series 2, and *The
Significant Death of Quentin Crisp* (Presenter), a
documentary for Channel Four.

Tim was Literary Manager of the Bush Theatre, London,
from 1997-2001.

MIKE BRADWELL
(Director of the original
Bush Theatre Production)

Mike trained at E15 Acting School. He played Norman in
Mike Leigh's award-winning film *Bleak Moments*, was
an actor/musician with the Ken Campbell Roadshow and
an Underwater Escapologist with Hirst's Carivari. He
founded Hull Truck Theatre Company in 1971 and
directed all their shows for ten years including his own
plays *Oh What, Bridget's House, Bed of Roses, Ooh La
La!, Still Crazy After All These Years* and new plays by
Doug Lucie, Alan Williams and Peter Tinniswood.

Mike has directed 30 shows at the Bush Theatre, London,
including *Hard Feelings* by Doug Lucie; *Unsuitable for
Adults* by Terry Johnson; *The Fosdyke Sagas* by Bill Tidy
and Alan Plater; *Love and Understanding* by Joe Penhall
(also at The Long Wharf Theatre, USA); *Love You, Too*
by Doug Lucie; *Dead Sheep* and *Shang-a-Lang* by
Catherine Johnson (also 1999 national tour); *Howie the*

Rookie by Mark O'Rowe (also Civic Theatre, Tallaght; Andrew's Lane Theatre, Dublin; 1999 Edinburgh Festival; Plymouth Theatre Royal; The Tron, Glasgow; PS122, New York; and the Magic Theatre, San Francisco); *Dogs Barking* by Richard Zajdlic; *Normal* by Helen Blakeman; *Resident Alien* by Tim Fountain (also for New York Theatre Workshop); *Flamingos* by Jonathan Hall and *Blackbird* by Adam Rapp.

He has also directed new plays by Helen Cooper, G.F. Newman, Jonathan Gems, Richard Cameron, Flann O'Brien and Terry Johnson at Hampstead Theatre, the Tricycle, King's Head, West Yorkshire Playhouse, Science Fiction Theatre of Liverpool, The National Theatre of Brent, The Rude Players of Winnipeg and the Royal Court, where he was Associate Director.

Mike has written and directed for television including *The Writing on the Wall; Games Without Frontiers; Chains of Love* and *Happy Feet* (BBC Screen One).

He is Artistic Director of the Bush Theatre.

JULIAN McGOWAN
(Designer)

Julian McGowan trained at the Central School of Art and Design. His recent design work includes: *Feelgood* (Garrick Theatre), *I Just Stopped by to See the Man* (Royal Court); *Mr Kolpert* and *Toast* (Royal Court Upstairs); *Single Spies*, *Enjoy* and *Blast from the Past* (West Yorkshire Playhouse); *Four Nights at Knaresborough* (New Vic at Tricycle Theatre); *Some Explicit Polaroids* (Out of Joint); *Waiting for Godot* (Royal Exchange Theatre, Manchester); *Our Lady of Sligo* (Out of Joint/Royal National Theatre/New York), *Our Country's Good* (Out of Joint/Young Vic); *The Censor* (Finborough

Theatre/Duke of York's/Ambassadors); *Blue Heart* (Out of Joint/Edinburgh Festival/Royal Court/national and international tour); *Shopping and Fucking* (Out of Joint/Ambassadors/West End and international tour); *The Steward of Christendom* (Brooklyn Academy of Music, New York); *Simply Disconnected* (Minerva, Chichester); *Translations* (Abbey Theatre, Dublin); *Hamlet* (Greenwich Theatre and tour); *An Experiment with an Air Pump* (Royal Exchange Manchester/Hampstead Theatre) and *Positive Hour* (Hampstead Theatre/Out of Joint).

His other design work for the theatre includes: *Don Juan*, *The Lodger* and *Women Laughing* (Royal Exchange Theatre, Manchester); *The Possibilities*, *The LA Plays* (Almeida), *Making History* (Royal National Theatre); *Heart Throb* (Bush); *Prin* (Lyric Hammersmith/West End); *Leonce and Lena* (Sheffield Crucible); *The Rivals*, *Man and Superman*, *Playboy of the Western World*, *Hedda Gabler* (Citizens' Glasgow); *Imagine Drowning* and *Punchbag* (Hampstead Theatre); *Tess of the D'Ubervilles* (West Yorkshire Playhouse); *The Changeling* and *The Wives' Excuse* (Royal Shakespeare Company); *A Doll's House* (Theatr Clwyd); *Torquato Tasso* (Edinburgh Festival); *American Bagpipes* and *The Treatment* (Royal Court), *Three Sisters*, *The Break of Day* and *The Steward of Christendom* (Royal Court/Out of Joint); *Old Times* (Theatr Clwyd/West End); *Cleopatra*, *Total Eclipse* and *A Tale of Two Cities* (Greenwich Theatre).

His opera designs include: *Cosi Fan Tutte* (New Israeli Opera); *Eugene Onegin* (Scottish Opera) and *Siren Song* (Almeida Opera Festival).

SID HIGGINS
(Lighting Designer)

Sid was a member of the National Youth Theatre prior to joining the company professionally as resident stage manager at the Shaw Theatre. After leaving the company, he developed his stage management career both on tour and in the West End, working on a wide range of productions in drama, musical theatre, opera and dance, including: Danny La Rue's *Dazzling Roadshow* (national tour); Wayne Sleep's *Dash* (national tour); *The Good Old Days* (national tour); *The Boy Friend* (Old Vic, Manchester Palace and Albery Theatres); the Royal National Theatre's production of *Guys and Dolls* (national tour and Prince of Wales Theatre); Kent Opera's productions of *The Barber of Seville, La Traviata* and *Agrippina* (national tour); Opera Northern Ireland's productions of *Don Giovanni, La Bohème, Faust* and *The Seraglio*. He has also worked on *The Vortex* (Garrick Theatre), *Les Miserables* (Barbican and Palace Theatres) and *Follies* (Shaftesbury Theatre).

Technical Management work includes *A Clockwork Orange* (Royalty Theatre)*; The Music Of Andrew Lloyd Webber* (Prince Edward Theatre and London Palladium); *Anything Goes* (Prince Edward Theatre); *The Phantom of The Opera* (Her Majesty's Theatre) and *Aspects of Love* (Prince of Wales Theatre) and several seasons with the National Youth Theatre to which he regularly returns.

General Management work includes *Song and Dance* (national tour); *The Hunting of the Snark* (Prince Edward Theatre); *Which Witch* (Piccadilly Theatre); The Complete Works of William Shakespeare (Criterion Theatre and two national tours); *The Bible - The Complete Word of God* (Gielgud Theatre); *Once On This Island* (Royalty Theatre); *90 Years of Dance* (Britton Theatre); *Think No Evil Of Us – My Life With Kenneth*

Williams (National Tour); *Cyrano de Bergerac* (Lyric Theatre); *Issey Ogata -City Life* (Lyric Theatre); *Trainspotting* (Tour); *Shopping and Fucking* (Gielgud and Queen's Theatres, national tour and New York Theatre Workshop); *The Snowman* (Peacock Theatre) and *Something Wonderful* (national tour) which he also designed.

He toured the United States with Vuka Uzibuze and Celtic Rhythm. He has also worked on many productions at the Edinburgh Festival. He designed *Age Sex Loc@tion* for the National Youth Theatre (Lyric Theatre Hammersmith and Podwil Theater in Berlin) and was lighting designer for *Puppetry of the Penis* (Whitehall Theatre and national tour).

Sid is now General Manager for the National Youth Theatre of Great Britain.

Quentin Crisp on Quentin Crisp

Quentin Crisp was reluctantly born on Christmas day in 1908. To his dismay he found himself to be the son of middle-class, middle-brow, middling parents who lived in Sutton, a suburb of London, England. After an uneventful childhood he was sent between the ages of 14 and 18 to a school in Derbyshire which was like a cross between a monastery and a prison. There he learned nothing that could ever be useful in adulthood except how to bare injustice. His ignorance of everything but this and his ambiguous appearance made a career impossible in anything except the arts. He therefore became an illustrator and designer of book covers. When he could no longer bare constantly being given the sack he tried freelancing but this was no more successful. At length, almost by chance he stood in for a friend who was an art-school model and finding that effort didn't cause him to collapse he took up posing as a career. With this way of life he struggled on for thirty five years. In the middle 1960s on a British radio channel to which no one listens he uttered a few words that led to his being invited to write his autobiography, *The Naked Civil Servant,* the synopsis of which caused the man who had commissioned it to faint dead away but another firm Jonathan Cape agreed to publish it in 1968. This is an offer Mr Crisp could not refuse because he was paid in advance. Upon becoming a resident alien of the United States in 1981 he moved to New York City vowing never to leave. Having been unsuccessfully a teacher of tap dancing, an occasional writer, and a minor televisionary, in the Winter of his life he described himself on his income tax forms as a retired waif. He died in 1999 just as this show reached the stage.

RESIDENT ALIEN

To Mike and Bette
and Nathan and David
with love and thanks

ACT ONE

Autumn 1999. Late morning.

Quentin Crisp's room, 46 East 3rd Street, New York.

The room is tiny and filthy. Piles of letters, papers, books, and objects around the floor. A single bed with a pile of scarves piled neatly at the foot of it. A tatty armchair. A heavy, old fashioned porcelain sink against one wall. Beneath it are old bottles and used paint containers. Underneath the two windows is an old 'baby belling' type stove utterly coated in grease. On the wall there is a photocopied, handwritten 'Reserved Quentin' sign, clearly a memento from some opening night. His trademark hat and scarf sits on the hook by the mirror. There is a narrow corridor leading to the door onto the landing. Halfway down it there is a chest of drawers covered with bottles of make-up and numerous other dubious looking potions.

Sunlight streams in through the stained net curtains. On the bed there is a 'hump' and from this 'hump' we now hear the sound of studio applause coming from a portable TV. We then hear a woman speaking.

WOMAN. I've been with my partner for five years and though we once loved each other deeply all the love has now gone from our lives but I can't free myself from him. What should I do?

QUENTIN. Kill him.

*The TV is suddenly turned off and the light under the sheet
extinguished. Quentin tosses back the sheet. He is wearing
a dirty dressing gown and has a small portable television
between his legs. He slides the television onto the cardboard
box it came in many moons ago.*

QUENTIN. I must wean myself off Miss Winfrey. Don't
get me wrong I admire her hugely, she must be one of
the richest women in the world and she came from
absolutely nothing but now we don't just get her in the
late morning but we get her in the afternoon and in the
middle of the night too embracing a lot of squishy
women. It used to be thought that you had to have talent
in order to achieve fame but television has changed all
that. We can now see that there are people in our society
who can earn vast sums of money, become the world's
sweethearts, be photographed at airports and be known
by name to the proprietors of hotels without displaying
talent of any kind. Even so it would be fruitless to try
and limit television's influence. However at the very least
it should be treated like Chinese rape. As it is inevitable
we should relax and enjoy its influence upon our lives.
This would at least have the effect of calling the bluff of
newscasters. The spreading of shocking news is not a
denunciation of war and so-called evils, it is a way of
selling television sets. It is a parallel activity with the
making of pornographic films.

Looked at from the front, the television screen appears
to be a lighted rectangle full of celebrities and other
disasters. Seen from behind, it is an arid waste in which,
like farmers in a dust bowl, broadcasters and producers
dig for something, anything on which to feed their
bleating flocks. Television has so much spare time that
everyone will be on it in the end. When you go on TV, as
you will because Mr Warhol has promised everyone his
fifteen minutes, you should treat your appearance like a

geography exam. The night before your exam you open
your Atlas at random and if it says China you learn
everything there is to know about China and if the next
day the main question in your paper is France, your
answer begins France is not like China. In television
terms that means if you've arrived with a wonderful
anecdote about your Mother and some clot asks about
your Father you reply Father's worn out coping with my
Mother WHO . . . You say what you have come to say
no matter what.

Remember that on television only one law prevails: The
survival of the glibbest. If your interviewer asks the
question, 'What is the secret of the universe?' you do not
stutter, you do not hesitate, above all you do not say
'a good question.' You say with a gracious smile, 'I am
happy to tell you there is no secret.' The remark is inane
but you are smiling and your lips are moving: you'll be
back.

He checks his watch.

Talking of inane remarks. I have people coming at one.
A couple from London, a Mr Brown and a Mr Black. A
most unfortunate co-junction of names. Anyway, they
wish to take me to lunch and to record my thoughts on
'how to be happy' afterwards on a tape recorder so that it
can be put on the Internet for the whole world to access.
I said to them that's like receiving advice from a doctor
who is more ill than you are, they laughed, in unison.

I think secretly Mr Brown and Mr Black hope I will die
soon and this web site will become some kind of virtual
obituary. I shall take great pleasure in denying them.
My agent says that I should stop meeting everyone who
calls and I should remove my name from the telephone
book. What is the use of a telephone if my number is

unlisted? It means that no-one will ever be able to call me. Think of the expense. I do occasionally get crank phone calls. I received one at four o'clock in the morning last week from a totally unknown caller who wanted to know if I had ever suffered from venereal disease and whether I knew Miss Garbo had died. I answered 'no' to the first question and 'yes' to the second. The stranger then said with a wistful intonation, 'I suppose that means we shall all die.' It does. And I received a very angry one from a member of the 'homosexual community' who said I was a twisted old queer who should die a horrible death after my comments about the 'People's Princess'. You see I lost the love of all the homosexual men in America in a single night when I said that I thought Princess Diana was trash and got what she deserved. She was Lady Diana before she was Princess Diana so she knew the racket. She knew that Royal Marriages have nothing to do with love. You Marry a man and you stand beside him on public occasions and you go like this (*He waves.*) and for that you never have a financial worry until the day you die. And everywhere you go you are photographed. What more does a woman want? English kings have always behaved badly. William IV had ten illegitimate children. Queen Adelaide would never have divorced him. Edward VII behaved so outrageously with his little friends that the English public knew their names. Lillie Langtry, Mrs Cornwallis-West, Rosa Lewis, but Queen Alexandra would never have divorced him and when he lay dying she said, 'Let Mrs Keppel be sent for.' Now isn't that wonderful? She was just as beautiful as Princess Diana and she was the Queen Of England and she was his wife and she knew she didn't matter. What gave Diana the idea that she mattered? My agent went mad, my editor said, 'You are so nice to people and then you go and say this.' My publisher said, 'If you think this will sell books you are very much mistaken.' I said you

don't understand. I don't say things to be liked, I say
them because I mean them.

He picks up a pile of correspondence from under his pillow.

Latterly I have become a kind of mail-order guru. People
write to me and people come and see me from all over
the world. Most of the people who come and see me are
very young indeed. And I know why they visit me - it's
in order to get the edge on their parents. I recently met a
girl of fifteen, she got me to write my name on a piece
of paper and the moment I stopped she said I can't make
up my mind whether to show this to my Mother or not.
She was going to save it for her darkest hour when her
Mother says, 'You dress yourself like a harlot, you do
nothing that your Father wishes, you use this house as a
hotel', and she's going to say, 'You don't know the half
of it Mother. I've met Quentin Crisp.' The other people
who come to see me are women in middle life, and over
and over again they ask me the same burning question:
'Is there life after marriage?' The answer is no. The
constant proximity of another person will cramp your
style in the end, unless that person is somebody you love
and then the burden will become unbearable at once.
How can anybody begin each dawn with a fresh assault
on his lifestyle if the moment he opens his eyes he hears
a voice beside him saying 'and another thing'. In my
opinion you must concentrate on yourself and
synthesising your professional and personal lives. Take
Joan Crawford, she appeared in any number of movies in
which she rose from rags to riches. In real life she finally
married Mr Pepsi Cola and she had all the luck in the
world because he died. That meant she could enter the
boardroom of that vast multinational empire where
presumably she said 'who told you to read the minutes'
just as she had done in all her movies. I once saw her at
the National Film Theatre in London. A car as long as

the Thames drew up and out stepped those two now
famous children. They stood in the lobby looking
bewildered and no wonder because after about three
minutes she came out of the same car and kissed the
children as though she hadn't seen them for months. She
was radioactive with belief in herself.

Excuse me. I must put on my 'going out' clothes for my
meeting. I preserve them you see. When I am here I am
'off' and I wear nothing but my filthy dressing gown.
This room is my dressing room and the world is my stage.
I haven't bought any new clothes since I came to
America eighteen years ago. In the matter of clothes
I am like a hospital, supported entirely by voluntary con-
tributions. It's true, whenever I am introduced to anyone,
however interested in other parts of their bodies I might
be, I always look first at their feet to see if theirs are as
small as mine. The trouble with shoes is that they are
unalterable. All other clothes I accept indiscriminately.
When I got to America I hoped I would die before my
shoes wore out. I never dreamed I would live as long as
I have. But now my entire wardrobe is threadbare and
I am threadbare too.

He takes off his dressing gown to reveal his bandaged body.

Apologies for my appearance but because of my eczema
large parts of my body have to be swathed in these
wretched bandages to prevent me from clawing myself
until the blood gushes out of my wounds and down the
stairs with a gurgling sound. Mr Eliot wrote that it is
'love that weaves the intolerable shirt of flame' but I'm
wearing it and I think it's eczema.

He puts his shirt on.

Oh and my left hand is now paralysed so I can no longer get my arm in my shirt as I would like. It also prevents me from typing which restricts the amount of publications I can contribute to. I write for only one newspaper now, the Manchester Guardian and there a man called Hattenstone rings me once a month and asks me what I have been doing and where I have been and when I tell him he says, 'I'll put you onto the copy department', and there there is a women who types so fast that she can type faster than I can speak and she gets it all down and they send a cheque.

People ask why I still work at ninety and I say because I need the money and they say, 'But you can't possibly need the money', but I do. You see when I lived in England my old age was taken care of by Mrs Snatcher. When the day came when I could no longer see or hear or walk she would spread her iron wings over me. Mrs Thatcher ascended the throne during one of my early exploratory visits to America. At that time hardly an evening passed without someone asking me my opinion of England's Prime-Minister. I thought and still think she was a star and I repeatedly said so. I once gave a talk and said as much and afterwards a young woman tackled me in the street and said, 'I hope you realise you gave all the wrong answers.' When my humble apologies finally subsided, she added, 'You are supposed to be against Mrs Thatcher'. I was obviously expected to take politics seriously – I never have. Of course if I had been born in China, Russia or Cuba I would have been shot. Then as I stood before the line of rifles I would have said 'hold your fire, I want to vote'. In Britain going to the polls is a waste of time. There are really only two factions; The Tories and the Labourites and whichever is in power it doesn't take long for people to start moaning what went wrong with the Labour (or Conservative) party? It came to power: that's what went wrong. The question is as pointless as asking, 'What went wrong with our marriage?' We got married; that's what went wrong. Politics are not an instrument for effecting social change, they are the art of making the inevitable appear to be a matter of wise human choice. Politics are not for people, they are for politicians - a medium in which a person can suspend his monstrous ego. The only benefit that can be derived by ordinary mortals from any of these vocations is that they provide us with someone on whom we can focus our attention - even our passions- at least in a manner less fatuous than soccer. It is this human need that Mr Disraeli, Mr Lloyd George, Mr Churchill and Mrs Thatcher fulfilled so well. It was amazing, she ruled the world and she was a woman. It's just a shame she couldn't have stayed a woman. When you become a king, the President or the Prime Minister you have to find a way of telling people why everything in the shops just got dearer and while you tell them you have got to smile. To me the great political stylist of all time was Mrs Eva Peron. In England spelling primers begin with the words 'the cat sat on the mat' - no wonder literacy is at such a low ebb when the first glimpse of it is this banal and even distasteful piece of information. But in Argentina spelling books began 'I love Evita'. And the crowning moment of her entire career was when she stood up in her box at the Opera House in Buenos Aires to make a speech. She lifted her hands to the crowd and as she did so, with a sound like railway trucks in a siding, the diamond bracelets slid down from her wrists. When the expensive clatter had died away her speech began 'we the shirt less'. And yet the Argentineans believed so much in Mrs Peron that when she died they petitioned the Pope to make her a Saint. His holiness declined but if he had consented what a triumph for political style that would have been. A double fox stole, ankle strap shoes and eternal life, nobody's ever had that before. The trouble with politics is it makes children believe that the perpetual violent turmoil of the world is soluble and this means they grow up with this terrible feeling that the world has been mismanaged by their parents, and that they must change it. Therefore they either take jobs where they can opt out entirely, or have the view that they should all go out to the middle of Biafra, and this to my mind is bad. There are situations which cannot be resolved; there are questions for which there are no answers and if you don't accept this then you will rapidly develop a police mentality. You will search for culprits, you will tear up contradictory evidence and you will push people around until they are in easily labelled and easily controlled blocs. Zealots are totally incapable of any emotion other than rage. It is an unalterable law that people who claim to care about the human race are utterly indifferent to the sufferings of individuals. I think some way must be found of getting the children to realise they live in an imperfect world, that there are no political systems which will make a difference. In fact, I would try and get children to see that politics is a complete waste of time and education is a last wild effort on the part of the authorities to prevent an overdose of leisure from driving the world mad. Learning is no longer an improver: it is merely the most expensive time filler the world has ever known. If when you peer into your soul you find that you are ordinary, then ordinary is what you must remain, but you must be *so* ordinary that you can imagine someone saying 'come to my party and bring your humdrum friend' and everyone knowing that he means you.

He resumes getting ready.

As I say, I have to go on working because in America there will be no-one to pick me up off the streets or pay my pension. It is the way of the country. I have found there is a strange relationship between the system of a country

and its people. In England the people are hostile to a man
but the system is benevolent. The very old, the very young
and the ill equipped to live will always be looked after. In
America everyone is friendly – almost doggie-like but
the system is ruthless. Once you can be pronounced
unproductive, you've had it. You will end up living in a
cardboard box at the corner of a street where once you
occupied a mansion. That is the reason why I live in this
one room in the last rooming house in New York . . .

   *We hear the roar of a large posse of motorbikes going up
   the street.*

On the same block as a group of Hell's Angels. I call
them my angels. Don't worry: they have a bad reputation
but they've never murdered me. My mode of living only
represents poverty to Americans - not to me. I live in
exactly the same way I lived in London in a room which
has not been dusted for eighteen years. After the first four
years it doesn't get any worse. It's just a question of not
losing your nerve. You will be surprised how the dust
accumulates. It does not lay on the surfaces you use
most. It does not lie in the path between the door and the
fire or the door and the stove, it's like snow, it drifts into
the corners of the room. Someone once asked me how I
kept the dust off my black velvet suit. I told them I jump
in the air when I put my trousers on.

   He puts his trousers on . . . Without jumping in the air.

I lied.

   He accidentally stands on a dirty plate.

And I don't wash up either. You see there's no need to
wash up unless you find you have passed the fish barrier.

It works like this, when you're hungry and you look at your plate and it says bacon you eat an egg and the next day when it says egg you think I could eat a fish. But when you've eaten a fish you have to wash up. I'm only saying these things so as to set you free from these boring domestic chores, so as to give you some time during each day when you stop looking outward and start looking inwards so as to decide who you truly are.

Starts to apply his make-up.

This is an ideal spot.

We hear someone above closing their door and footsteps coming down the stairs.

There are three floors. I am on the second. I share a bathroom in the hallway with my neighbours. There is a Super, his name is 'Happy Phace'. He is a very tall, part-time drag queen who is very kind and lets me in when I forget my keys which happens quite often. He has a Chihuahua which since it won the Taco-Bell advertisement on television has been insufferable and barks every time I go onto the landing.

A dead mouse is pushed through the letter box.

Oh and there is a gentleman above who insists on putting dead mice under my door as a token of his esteem.

Quentin totters to the door and picks it up.

He stopped for a while when the young lady below acquired a cat and he ran out of ammunition, unfortunately she has moved on.

He pops the mouse in a bin.

I am living under 'mouse arrest'.

He puts on a 'stars and stripes' diamante brooch around his neck scarf.

I have always been American in my heart ever since my mother took me to the movies in South Wimbledon. She took me to the cinema in a spirit of ostentatious condescension, the movies were for 'serving gals', people with any taste went to the theatre. But when I saw the pictures of New York on the screen I began to gibber and twitch. My Mother said that what went on in the screen was vastly different from what happened in real life, but she was wrong because everyone who comes to New York from London and goes back says one thing: 'It's more like the movies than you'd ever dreamed.' And it is: they really do bring the dining-room tables onto the pavement in the summer and they mop their necks with Kleenex and they say, 'It isn't the heat it's the humidity.' I was standing at a bus stop on 3rd Avenue and a black gentleman went by and when he saw me he said, 'Well my, you've got it all on today.' And he was laughing and I laughed and I had got it all on. When I was swanning around the West End with all the other young boys on the game in the thirties, I thought what a pity it is we never look at one another, we never smile. It could all be one long party, and in Manhattan it is one long party.

I longed to leave England after I had grown up and had been subjected to the hostility of the English. I don't ever remember a time when I was not being laughed at. But the time comes for everybody when he has to do deliberately what he used to do by mistake, this is the only way by which you can get the joke onto your own terms. I did this from twenty one or twenty two onwards,

I made it clear that I knew what it was they were
laughing at and this made my life much easier to bear.
It lessened the tension between me and other people.
This is, in my view, the beginning of your own style.
It's funny because when the law was changed regarding
homosexuality in Britain people said, 'It will make a
great difference to you.' I said it will make no difference
to me. No one pointed at me and said, 'Look at him he's
illegal', they said 'he's effeminate'. That was my sin. You
see the English don't like effeminate women. English
men are always saying 'oh she's such a nuisance she's
always fiddling with her appearance and asking what she
looks like'. American men encourage that. An American
man calls his girlfriend 'sugar, honey, baby'. An English
man calls his wife 'old girl'. Who wants to be an old
girl? Someone wrote to me recently and said, 'You are a
sad, lonely embittered old queen who isn't interested in
anything that interests anyone else' and I thought, 'That's
right.' Apart from the loneliness. I'm not lonely. Besides
I have to live alone. I haven't room for anyone else with
all the books I receive. At least three a week.

Of course I try never to read them. Books are for writing
not for reading but they pursue me from all angles.
Authors send me the books they have written. (I don't
think English authors ever do that, it would seem
immodest.) Then there are the magazines which will send
you books with a covering note telling you how many
words to write about them and what you will be paid.
They go to the top of the pile. And then there are
publishers who send you uncorrected proof copies of
books they intend to market with a letter that says, 'We
are sure you will enjoy this book and hope you will share
your enthusiasm with us.' That means 'say something
nice that we can put on the back of the first edition.
Do not expect to be paid'. These go to the bottom of the
pile. So you see there isn't room for anyone else.

He looks out the window.

Oh no. It's coming onto snow . . .

The closest I ever came to living with someone was fifty-odd . . . no, sixty-odd years, years ago. He was the size of a barn door and as easily pushed to and fro. He formed the habit of visiting me every weekend and my life became a series of Saturdays for which I prepared and Sundays from which I recovered, but I never gave up hope. I never let more than a few hours pass without including in the conversation the words 'When you have a room of your own,' and I never gave him a latch key. I knew that once I had done that, I was a lifer. When presumably to normalise our relationship, he suggested a little sex, I concurred. A year or so later, in the middle of a sketchy embrace, he said, 'Let's pack this in.' I said 'Let's'. You see if you are going to have a relationship between two people one of you will inevitably adopt the part of the stooge, one of you will be left expressing amazement and amusement at jokes you have heard a thousand times. When I say you must lie alone I am not trying to curtail your sex lives, all I am trying to do is snatch the straw from your beak and prevent all this nesting. If you share a territory you will, in the end, only be left with the things about which you disagree. If you get up at six o'clock and your little friend gets up at six in the morning within a week you will take this for granted and you will say 'isn't it amazing, we agree'. But if your friend wants the soap on the left hand side of the wash basin and you want it on the right. Divorce! And people will say you got divorced over a cake of soap? But they forget that you moved it EVERY DAY!

Never get into a narrow double bed with a wide single man. Shortly before one Easter holiday I told him that it was time I visited my Mother for at least a weekend. He was deeply devoted to his Mother. He gathered up his things and left. And as he did so he said, 'I don't see what I've done wrong even now.' It was the saddest day of my life.

But then he married and had two children so he's one of my successes. I knew he was a Kinsey Queer rather than a coot queer. He merely associated with homosexuals because they bought their love by the pound. It's true. When two gay people meet in a bar and one tells the other about his new lover they don't ask 'how wise is he?', 'how funny is he?' they ask 'how big is it?'. If they'd just let sex go away just think of all the free time they'd have. He's dead now. In knowing him I came to know the whole world - there is no dark stranger.

The phone rings. Quentin answers it.

Oh yee-ees?

No response.

Hello? Hello? Hello?

They are cut off.

Judging from their difficulties with street telephones that will be my English visitors.

He goes to put his coat on.

The electricity in this building is so weak that it won't power the doorbell so people have to call me from the box on the corner to get me to let them in.

The phone rings again. He returns and answers it.

Hello? Hello. I'll run down now!

He puts the phone down and crosses to the mirror to put his hat on. He turns to the audience. He now looks like the Quentin Crisp we all know.

Excuse me, I have to go and tell two people who inhabit the dank, dark, prison of eternal love 'how to be happy'. I may be some time.

He leaves. We hear the chihuahua bark on the landing before the lights fade to black.

End of Act One.

ACT TWO

*Five minutes later. The room as before. Quentin enters in
his coat and hat. He carries an opened Fed-Ex parcel.*

QUENTIN. It wasn't them! It was the Fed-Ex man with
another book for endorsement. He's brought so many of
them here that he practically apologises when he gives
them to me. Maybe I should get him to do the
endorsements, cut out the middle man.

He picks up his magnifying glass and looks at the cover.

'Profiles in Gay and Lesbian Courage'.

*He tosses the book onto the bed with disdain. He places the
envelope with a pile of other Fed-Ex envelopes that he
seems to be collecting for some reason. He looks out of the
window. The snow is heavier.*

It's coming down in fifty dollar bills now. I do hope Mr
Brown and Mr Black are going to come. I daren't go out
alone on slippery or uneven surfaces; if I were to fall and
break even the smallest bone, it would never mend; I am
no longer renewable.

He sits on the bed and holds his chest.

Blessed angina . . . There ought to be a Ministry Of
Death you know, though in Orwellian terminology,
I suppose it would be named The Ministry Of Heaven.
It would be an august body of men all preferably under

thirty years of age who would deal with the chore of exterminating old people. Before everything else they would have to agree upon a limit (say sixty) to live beyond which would be an offence (punishable with life?) Then the Ministry would have to make sure that, six months before his sixtieth birthday, every living being received a notice of postdated congratulations advising him which town hall he would be required to visit on the happy occasion. A week before his final birthday he would receive a final notice and then, at the glorious hour, unless he preferred to walk there on his own two feet, the van would call to take him to oblivion. In America this vehicle would be painted to look like a fiery chariot but in England it would be plain blue with the words 'Ministry of Death, Kensington Branch' discreetly lettered on the side. For the first few years there might be undignified scenes, but in Britain individual liberty is so often curtailed for the common good that order would soon prevail. If the government does not soon adopt some plan such as I have outlined, I shall have to put into action a more personal scheme for limiting my span of years. I shall commit a murder. This is something that for a long time I have wanted to do. It would be impossible to get through the kind of life I have known without accumulating a vast stockpile of rage. Whenever people read in the papers that someone has purchased a machine gun and mowed down a whole neighbourhood, they invariably say, 'I wonder what brought that on'. They even make some such remark when the subject is an American Negro. To me the motive is self evident. Mass Murderers are simply people who have had ENOUGH! Someone once asked me to what I attributed my longevity and I replied, 'Bad luck.' It's true. I'm ready for death but I just won't die. I once sat opposite a little old lady in a train carriage near Bromley and overheard her say to someone ' . . . and then after twenty five years, my husband died'. I was just about to look gravely at the floor when she added 'and oh, the relief'. I understand her utterly.

We hear heavy metal music coming from above.

Particularly when the Mouse Man is playing his music. Music is a mistake. When I was young the world was silent. Well there were concerts but these took place in concert halls. A concert hall is like the gents, if you feel a certain need you go to the place and there you meet other people in the same predicament and if the place is properly constructed the stench of culture does not seep out into the street! But now music is everywhere. One cannot help asking 'of what were you afraid?' Why can't you bare the sound of the puff puffs on the station, why did you have to have the music? Why couldn't you bare the sound of the barber's clippers? Why have you reduced all human experience to one experience? The music. You've taken away all the variety that there used to be in life. And worse than that you've had to give up the speech. There is no point in trying speak and when you give up the words you give up the thoughts. With music we can only gibber and twitch!

We hear footsteps coming down the stairs.

Wait for it.

Another mouse is placed through the letter box. Quentin takes it from him before it can fall to the floor.

Thank you.

He pops it in the bin again. The phone rings. He answers it quickly, obviously expecting it to be Mr Brown and Mr Black.

Oh yee-ees. Yeas. Oh yeas. Oh dear. Oh well. Yes, yes,
yes do that. Call me after lunch. Goodbye.

He puts the phone down.

That was Mr Golner my agent!

He checks his watch. Then makes sure that he has replaced
the receiver properly and that it is actually 'on the hook'.
It is.

Maybe I offended Mr Brown and Mr Black with my
comments about Old Compton Street in London. You see
they live there and they asked me what I thought of it.
I have never liked ghettos. I once met a man at an airport
who said that the homosexuals of Minnesota are in
favour of the 'separate-but-equal' solution to their
problems. I said, 'Why?' He said, 'We don't have
anything in common with the straights.' What a peculiar
thing to say. They have everything in common except
their funny way of spending their evenings. If you only
talk about your sex life you will never have anything in
common with anyone. And this man's 'constant
companion' recalled that I had once declared that if Mr
Clinton announced that he was converting Indiana into a
reservation for homosexual people and that we must all
go and live there I would burst into tears. I still think
that. I would feel I was being starved of reality. If I think
about my life I see it as a slow journey from the outer
suburbs of ostracism almost to the heart of the world -
assuming it has a heart. I would not wish to be shunted
into a siding. The trouble with gay reservations is they
breed a terrible uniformity. They claim to be a place
where people can be themselves but very often that
involves the most boring form of camp which has
nothing to do with individual style and everything to do
with the fear of 'breaking ranks'.

The strange thing about camp is that it has become
fossilised. The mannerisms have never changed. It
remains the same now as it did when I first walked along
Piccadilly and Shaftesbury Avenue as a young man. Then
you had men stood on street corners who said 'isn't it
terrible tonight dear. No men about, The dilly's not what
it used to be'. Then you'd get the mannequin walk and
the stance in which the hip was only prevented from total
dislocation by the hand placed upon it. The whole set of
stylizations that are known as camp, was in 1926 self
explanatory. Women moved and gesticulated in this way.
Homosexuals wished for obvious reasons to copy them.
If I were now to see a woman sitting with her knees
clamped together, one hand on her hip and the other
lightly touching her back hair, I should think either
she scored her last social triumph in 1926 or it is a man
in drag.

We spent all our time in Old Compton Street in those
days huddled together in a café called the Black Cat. Day
after uneventful day, night after loveless night we sat in
this café buying each other cups of tea, combing each
other's hair and trying on each other's lipsticks. We could
make each cup of tea last as long as a four-course meal.
Of course the owner occasionally threw us out. When
this happened we waltzed around the neighbouring
streets in search of love or money or both. If we didn't
find any we returned to the café to put on more lipstick.
It never occurred to any of us to try and be more lovable.
Even if it had I don't think we would have adopted a
measure so extreme. Occasionally whilst we chatted one
of our friends would go whizzing past crying, 'They're
coming'. At this we would scatter. It meant that while
being questioned one of the boys had bolted and his
inquisitors were after him. At such times if a detective
saw his quarry escaping, he would seize upon the nearest
prey, however innocently that person might be behaving.

We treated the police as it is said you should treat wild dogs. As we passed them we never ran but if they were already running, we spread out so only one of our number would die. The perpetual danger in which we lived bound us together. In the café there was a lot of stylised cattiness but this was never unkindly meant. When we were not thus engaged, we talked about our sufferings and this I greatly preferred. Soon I learned by heart every argument that could be raised in the climate of that time against the persecution of homosexuals. We weren't doing any harm, we couldn't help it, and though this was hardly water tight from a legal point of view, we had enough to bear already. Courtship consisted of walking along the street with a man who had my elbow in a merciless grip until we came to a dark doorway. Then he said 'this'll do'. These were the only words of tenderness that were ever uttered to me. By heterosexuals the life after death is imagined as a world of light, where there is no parting. If there is a heaven for homosexuals, which doesn't seems very likely, it will be very poorly lit and full of people they can feel pretty confident they'll never have to meet again.

The life of a homosexual is so horrible that when I was young I couldn't believe it. It's not the social persecution it's what you are expected to do. I swanned around the West End looking wonderful and I thought, 'Oh I'm marvellous,' I didn't think what I had to do at the end of it. And when I learned I was so horrified would have gone into a monastery. Does anyone want to take someone's penis into his mouth? It's so disgusting I couldn't bare it. Ohhh! Marlene Dietrich said you have to let them put it in otherwise they won't come back. Isn't that wonderful? She wanted praise not sex. Sex smudges your make-up. You see it's been explained to me at the age of 90 that I am not really a homosexual, I am a trans something or other, I can't remember what. I'm a woman in a man's body. If they'd had the operation to have *it* chopped off when I was younger I should have become a woman and I should have opened a knitting shop in Carlisle and no-one need ever have known my guilty secret and I should have been happy because I should have been part of life. The trouble with homosexuals is they are always *pretending* to live, they don't *actually* live.

Looks at his watch.

One thirty. It appears my guests are not coming and the Worldwide Web is to be spared my thoughts on 'how to be happy'. It's ironic because one of the things I should have told my visitors is that it is an excess of freedom that makes modern man so unhappy and here they are exercising it by not turning up.

He takes off his coat.

I do believe it's true though. When modern man looks round in search of a destiny nothing presents itself to him as it did when I was young as being suited to his age, his class, his station. Instead he sees a landscape without signposts, the sheer vastness of the terrain that lies before him overwhelms him. I come from a time when there was so little liberty that if a girl wanted to wear nail varnish she had to leave home for good and if a man wore suede shoes . . . then there was nothing for him to do but join the Foreign Legion. Now people have got all this freedom and yet wherever I look people are not rejoicing, they are complaining or in therapy or both. I know it's too late to ask them to abide by laws handed down by their pasters and masters and elders and betters but what we need are chains. Chains of our own making. However heavy these may be they will never feel as

irksome as limitations placed on us by others. We have to
have a system and that begins with each of us trying to
decide what it is that makes him the way he is. It
involves a journey to the interior - not an altogether
pleasant experience because as well as totting up what
you consider to be your assets you also have to take a
long look at what your friends call 'the trouble with you'
and the synthesis between these two opposite opinions
will be your identity.

He gets a potato.

You have to polish up your raw identity until it becomes
a lifestyle.

*He picks up a knife and puts the potato on the plate and sits
on the bed.*

Something interesting by which you are proud to be
identified and something with which you can do barter
with the outer world to get from it what you want.
I won't say what you deserve because if we all got what
we deserve we would starve.

He starts to peel his potato.

Many people say, 'I'm not wealthy enough to be stylish.'
But you will not need wealth. There was a woman in
Soho many years ago, a woman known as The Countess
and in spite of this she had in fact no fixed address and
no means of support and her body was perpetually bent
double from a life long habit of looking in dustbins and
one day in an expensive part of London she found a
complete backless beaded dress. She longed for dusk to
fall so that she could nip into a dark doorway and try it
on. Round about half past six her patience had worn out

she went into a churchyard in the middle of London and there she proceeded to take off her clothes. This caused a crowd to collect and the crowd caused a policeman to collect and the next day in court when the Magistrate said 'and what exactly were you doing stripping amongst the dead?' she replied 'I was doing what any women would be doing at that hour - changing for dinner'. So you see however grandiose the style you have chosen for yourself you will not even need any actual money to support it and more than that you won't even need talent.

Now I never saw Sarah Bernhardt on the stage but I have seen a strip of movie showing her coming into the home stretch in *Camille*. The death scene. She sits opposite Armand on a chaise longue wearing a minimum risk nightdress, with clowns make-up and her hair is right down into her eyes. Now someone must have told her it was a silent movie, but did she care? No, once the cameras started to turn her lips started moving faster than those of a policeman giving corrupt evidence and when her lips moved her eyes began to roll and when her eyes moved a hand shot out into the hair returning later to give her a terrible blow on the chest. Sometimes it was one arm, sometimes it was another, sometimes it was both arms together and then as abruptly as all this activity had began it stopped. Her arm swung down in front of the couch like the limb of a rag doll. Now I am not just trying foist on you my own Philistine reactions. This movie was shown at the National Film Theatre in London and that is a building to which no-one can obtain admission unless he can prove that he comes from the cheese and wine belts of England but it made no difference. The audience choked with derisive mirth, a man near me fell out into the gangway his feet twiddling in the air. 'La Divine' indeed, it wasn't her acting that made Miss Bernhardt divine, it was her nerve.

He plops the chopped potato in the water and turns on the
stove. The lights 'dip' momentarily.

Nowadays you don't even need virtue to have a lifestyle,
you no longer have to be an object of public veneration
or even affection, you can be the focus of contempt or
even downright hatred. After all as a test of whether you
are still in touch with someone else, being loved can
never be a patch on being murdered. That's when
someone really has risked his life for you. And if you
decide on depravity as the fluid in which you will
suspend your monstrous ego then you have the most
wonderful examples behind you. In Mediaeval France,
living at the same time as Joan Of Arc there was a great
French nobleman called Gilles De Rais and he murdered
a 150 choirboys in a lifetime. Now quantity is not style.
All the same it's difficult not to be impressed, isn't it?

But of course before you can build some dizzying,
dazzling structure as a monument to yourself you must
first get the foundations of your private life absolutely
solid. From now on you should have nothing at home
that doesn't represent the kind of person you have
decided to become. It doesn't matter if your house is full
of gadgets which are advertised on TV every twenty
minutes - they've got to go. And when you've got rid of
the superfluous things you start on the superfluous action.
From now onward there should be no doodling and
dawdling and I used to say there must be no day
dreaming but I've changed my opinion recently. I think
you are allowed your daydreams up to the age of twenty-
five, but after that they may become an alibi. Do you
understand me? It's no good running a pig farm badly for
thirty years, whilst saying really I was meant to be a
ballet dancer, by that time pigs will be your style. And it
follows logically if there's to be no doodling and
dawdling there's to be no evening classes. It's alright if

you are learning to sing or dance because these are activities the results of which you take out into the world and wear like a crown. People who have learned to sing will always have richer, rounder voices. People who've learned to dance will always have bigger, bolder movements, but as for pottery and basket weaving, what good are they? The moment the doors of the evening institute clang shut behind you you are back where you started. On the way home you might get into an argument with a stranger at a bus stop. It's no good saying I can't express myself you'll have to come and see my baskets.

Of course it's not enough merely to get the foundations of your life in order. You also have to decide what you are going to do in the outer world. Now some of you may be so old fashioned that you still have jobs. If this is so try not to get stuck in work where you only deal with things, and I include the highest level of things; sculpture, books, paintings, they are only objects just like washing machines but not so useful. It would be difficult to express the dilemma that lies before the visual artist. If I showed you a huge great piece of concrete with a hole in it everybody would say it's a Henry Moore, but if I could show you Henry Moore himself nobody would know who he was. So all that clipping, all that chipping, all that chiselling, it's been in vain.

The difficulty with establishing all this for yourself is we live in a world riddled with envy. People are always squeaking for equality. Equality is a dead word. Never desire to be anyone's equal. Once you have entered the profession of being, you have become a professor of a subject about which you are the only living authority. What other people do with their lives, with their style will not matter. Every morning say to yourself, prefer-ably aloud, 'Other people are a mistake!' No I withdraw that remark it might be thought sweeping. Say to yourself 'concern with other people is a mistake'. Now I know this is not what most people teach you but I am trying to spare you the traditional scramble for mutual self sacrifice. Altruism is a debilitating, fragmenting process but the constant watch over and the perfection of your idea of yourself and the presentation of it gift wrapped to others is a unifying and invigorating way of life and it carries with it a built-in invitation to the party at the end of the world, that glittering function at which everybody will be speaking but no-one will be listening. If you are armed with your style you will be able to run towards that happy hubbub without the faintest fear that you will be out of your depth. More important the burdens of your sorrowful and angry freedom, these problems of who to be and where to go and even what to think, they will fall away from you forever. Do not be the kind of person for whom the band is always playing in the other room. Develop a lifestyle. Ask yourself, 'If there were no praise, and no blame, who would I be then?' Then you know who you are, and what your style is. Oscar Wilde said in matters of great importance it is not sincerity that matters, but style, yet to me they are the same thing. Style is not a lot of dandyism or flourishes encrusted on your public image. It's a way of stripping yourself of everything but your true self so you can only judge the style by the content and you only reach the content through the style. As far as I'm concerned, people are always saying to me, 'All you want to be is noticed.' It isn't enough. I want to be recognised. My appearance is simply a leaflet thrust into the hands of astonished bystanders and this is the reason I think Mr Wilde fell apart. When he came out of gaol (and he'd only been there two years) he fell apart completely and spent the rest of his life in a drunken stupor in Paris. I've known people who were in prison twice as long without writing any of that bad verse, and when they came out of jail they went on with their lives, shaken, but they went on with their lives. But Mr Wilde must have accepted the judgment passed on him by society or else he would not have been crushed by it. One is left dazed by the discrepancy between the way he saw himself and the way anyone else would have seen him. First of all there was no need for him to bring a case against Mr Queensberry. Secondly he could have evaded the case and was advised to do so by his friends and when in court with the case going against him he continued pert replies and thirdly he dragged the fair name of Mr Plato into this sordid case. He was mentioning 'the love that dare not speak its name'. How can love be used in a case where the names of dozens of young men had been read out that Mr Wilde only met in braille? Procured for him by Lord Alfred Douglas and devoured behind closed curtains in a darkened room. He had no idea of just how sordid his life seemed to the rest of the world, he lived in a dream.

He goes to the fridge and opens it. It is empty apart from a single, solitary egg sitting on the shelf.

Who says life is devoid of possibility? Scrambled, boiled, poached or fried? Fried I think.

He takes the egg out and cracks it into the frying pan.

Why does the yolk always break!?

He fiddles with the egg but it is clearly sticking in the pan and turning into something of a mess.

My Agent says I should stop meeting everyone who calls, indeed I could now be sitting in the window of the café on 2nd Avenue enjoying a proper lunch, but he doesn't understand I've gone into the fame business. He

tells me that I can't just 'do' fame, but I can. Every day
through the mails I receive invites to Broadway theatre
first nights, to secret screenings of unpopular films, to the
opening of galleries exhibiting works by obscure artists
and to parties for someone no-one has ever heard of in
dim basements. I can't go to all of them but I must go to
some or they will cease to send the invitations and I shall
be cut off from the world. I cannot endow the wing of a
hospital or University I do not have the money, all I can
give to repay America for allowing me to be a Resident
Alien is my infinite availability. People are my only
pastime. I have taken my wages in them and while ever
they they take an interest in me I shall be a happy man.

*He puts his egg on the plate, scoops out some potatoes from
the pan and puts them alongside it. It all looks hideous. He
pours himself a huge whisky into a dirty glass and gets a
knife and fork and sits on the bed with the plate on his lap,
his glass on top of the TV.*

So today somebody failed to come. So be it. Someone
else will come tomorrow. If not, so be that. You see you
can only be lonely if you don't know what to do with the
time when you are alone and you walk around the room
thinking 'I am alone, no-one comes to see me I am
worthless'. What matters is not what other people think
about you but what you think about yourself. You must
not value love because it is requited. It makes no
difference whether your love is returned. Your love is of
value to you because you give it. It's as though you gave
me a present merely because you thought I would give
you one in return. This won't do. If you have love to
give, you give it and you give it where it is needed, but
never, never ask for anything in return. Once you've got
that in your head, the idea of your heart being broken
will disappear forever.

Neither look forward where there is doubt, nor backward where there is regret; Look inward and ask yourself not if there is anything out in the world that you want and had better grab quickly before nightfall, but whether there is anything inside you that you have not yet unpacked. Be certain that before you fold your hands and step into your coffin, what little you can do and say and be is completed.

The phone rings. He answers it.

Oh yee-es. Yes. Yes. Knowledge is a strong word but I do know a little about silent movie actresses, yes. Lunch would be lovely. I'll just get the Sacred Book.

He opens his diary.

Tomorrow looks perfect. One o'clock. Cooper Diner. It's in the book. Not at all, I exist to please.

He puts the phone down.

For sixty long years of my life the phone never rang. Now it rings *every* day. You were lucky to catch me in.

He holds his glass up in a toast.

To life! A funny thing that happens to you on the way to the grave.

He starts to eat. The lights fade to black.

The End.